FOOTNOTES FROM HISTORY
THE DEBORD VARIATIONS
COLIN CAMPBELL ROBINSON

Newton-le-Willows

Published in the United Kingdom in 2021
by The Knives Forks And Spoons Press,
51 Pipit Avenue,
Newton-le-Willows,
Merseyside,
WA12 9RG.

ISBN 978-1-912211-89-0

Copyright © Colin Campbell Robinson, 2021

The right of Colin Campbell Robinson to be identified as the author of this work has been asserted by them in accordance with the Copyrights, Designs and Patents Act of 1988. All rights reserved. No part of this publication may be reproduced, stored in a retrieval system, transmitted in any form or by any means, electronic, photocopying, recording or otherwise, without prior permission of the publisher.

Acknowledgements:

Parts of *Footnotes from History* have appeared in *Otoliths*, *The Gambler* and *Empty Mirror*.

'The Debord Variations' are based on Guy Debord's footnotes to his essay *Comments on the Society of the Spectacle* written in 1967.

FOOTNOTES FROM HISTORY
THE DEBORD VARIATIONS

to the everyday[1]

---
[1] *The dog dreams and sighs*
   The everyday
           – Emmanuel Hocquard

Footnotes From History

1.

Words ambushed, then condemned:
words hit, assassinated by assailants unknown.

A mysterious **trap:** such banditry on the streets of our capital.

Who is in the under**world**: under the **world** is **who**?

7

Colin Campbell Robinson

> *The **unhappiness** of the times:*
> *the times **unhappiness**.*

From then till **now**,
from   now till
   then

one measure for a half measure,
the half measure's enough to do the job.

   Half measures enough to make the hit.

Footnotes From History

He fell; no one caught him. How do you catch a falling man who is trapped?

An enigma without beginning and **a scene** without **an end,** conspire.

Colin Campbell Robinson

2.

Never has everything been so *disconnected*, he said.

The conditions for revolution are so ripe they've begun to rot, he added.

The crowd crowded in around the screen so as to *connect* with the event and *disconnect* with each other.

Every day is revolting: the revolution of every day.

Footnotes From History

Stalled by desire, false desire, but desire.

They want the ball; they want the game,
they want to sing and cry through *empty time*, he said,
and then left having spoken.

Colin Campbell Robinson

3.

Under a poor cloak you often find a good drinker.
– Cervantes

Fake wine for those who work as everything's for sale. In the dark, in the light, either are the same.

Who earns a living, who lives a living, who takes a living away.

Meanwhile, in the caves, torches flicker and there is movement but no dance.

Footnotes From History

Is this the **dream dreamt** on another shore
                                      long forgotten?

    To make a mark, make two under the sign of
the **beaten**.

Cobbled street carries the day's passage.

Few venture, rain lumbers across
    the placid sea,
    soon to kiss.

A glass is poured, hear the bubbling and the harp.

Colin Campbell Robinson

4.

Ghosts walk, ghosts talk:
    they're the only ones.

Hear the music, sphere music.

It's not that we're deluded, more that we're *diminished*.

Shine a **light** from the prison, shine a **light** from on high
    both understand the
        darkness.

Then the crowd cries **the sad moment** before defeat.

Is this no time?

Everyone knows **we've been told** but there is no **listening.**

The deaf are the new blind.

Colin Campbell Robinson

5.

men resemble their times more than their fathers
– **Arab proverb**

Circles are going around, return to the same place or different,
   with the same people, or different?

During the circuit things happen and when the circuit is retraced things happen
but are they the same things or different?

Footnotes From History

Someone recorded both circuits but they may
have tampered with the recordings.

    No-one is sure, no-one remembers anymore.

So who's fault is that, who's fault the recordings
are cut and pasted like so many circuits that no
longer connect.

How many fathers, how many sons, the circle is broken,
the circuit is jammed by the no time.

And here, in the ever present, the walls collide.

Colin Campbell Robinson

6.

Who is doing penance for the **revolution** that did not happen?

Who lost time waiting for a moment that **never comes**?²

The man on the island re-lives a rainbow, flies a kite.

Listen to the language spoken under modern conditions
                                                           of life.

[2.] The footnote for today remains what it is, a footnote.

Footnotes From History

He looks back and blames past time for the lack of future and unwraps the present he's been given.

This rich moment; this poor moment.

Cold audacity and the false report: there are witnesses.

Without importance, hostile manoeuvres doomed to failure.

The rigid beast outshines the angel-light.

Colin Campbell Robinson

No one forgives good counsel when they suffer the
results.

The **morsel of revolt** is harder to digest than history and the compromise.

Around this time he became exhausted
and so departed.

Too close to the *'actual'*.

Footnotes From History

7.

to be is to be guilty
– Samuel Beckett, *Stories and Texts for Nothing*

Innocence can't be proven; sentencing will always be for life.

Those presiding cover all tracks.

The charges remain opaque.

There is a waiting room but no exit.

Cells multiply below.

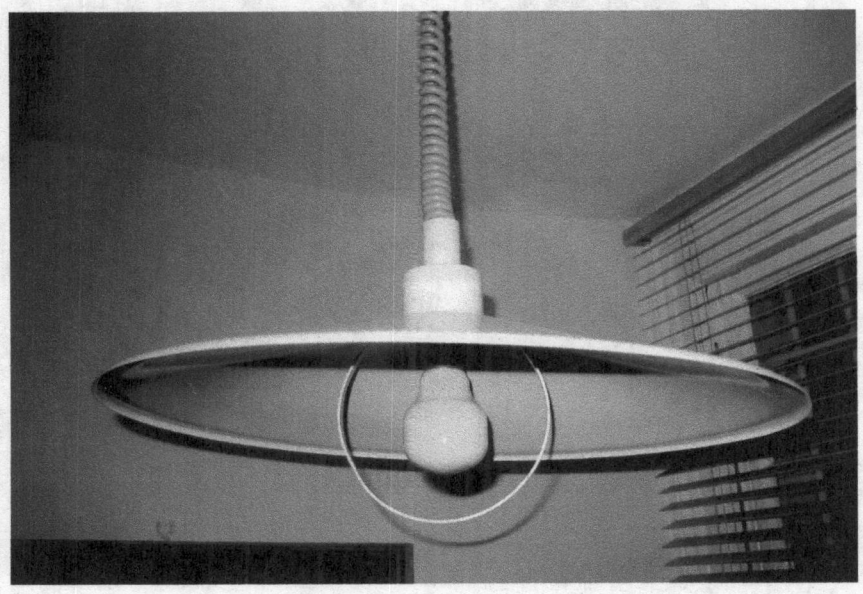

Colin Campbell Robinson

The duty sergeant is out to tea.
Keys have all been recut.

You have been summoned:

a knock
a strange humming
moon behind cloud.

This evening.

8.

Footnotes From History

In spite of so many trials, my experience and the grandeur of my task convinces me all is well.
– Robespierre

At this moment jailed, many years untried.

What have they done? What have we done? What has been done?

There was no motive therefore there is no rescue, he decried.

Colin Campbell Robinson

All of those *included* are not *included*. Those who *belong* do not *belong*.

There are other obstacles, the right of passage, and the payment on the hour.

And then there is the b
                            l
                       a
                         d
                            e.

Footnotes From History

9.

Guilt - culbabilite - colpa - schuld
Otherwise no results found.

The logic of his **guilt** clearly established
he confesses to a crime he knows he hasn't
committed.

Later in the day he retracts his statement.
All that is left are **empty words.**

Colin Campbell Robinson

The prosecutor knows the **judge,** knows the judgement.

Whereas the defence only knows the guiltless, only knows **the end**.

At four in the morning the **dreams scatter.**
                    What is left to say?

In the Romance languages guilt is feminine.

                She confesses.

10.

Footnotes From History

Seek veritas

        in discourse:

three parties
one abstains
no discourse
no verum.

If no **truth**
only evasions,

        only pretence.

Colin Campbell Robinson

Pretence can be play
but it also can be **lies:**

      four parties
      one lies
      one believes
      two repelled

Develop a theory of secrets:

      one hides
      one finds
      two chasing bubbles

Write fiction
as entertaining lies.

Lies *to make you happy*
is the title of this book.

Footnotes From History

Seek veritas through **struggle,** then in the last moment

resistance weakens,
collaboration strengthens,
reality slides.

three resistant
one betrays
two slowly fade from sight.

Collaboration can produce positive results but it can also herald the end.

Colin Campbell Robinson

four are in a room
two conspire
two are frozen out

The title of this book is
'as serious as your life'.

Footnotes From History

11.

Is it this, **the decline**, the fall?

Even those who strive not to **weaken** in the face,
not to **weaken** on the sand, **to travel** on,
forgetting.

To travel on to the end.

The medications given cannot cure; the
medications only make it worse.

Colin Campbell Robinson

And this is it, down the path, the ashes disperse and finally gone.

A moon gives off a full quavering. Such a **magic** realm revealed.

The marble swan flutters higher than necessary.

Only this evening and never repeated.

Footnotes From History

12.

Are **false hopes** better than **no hopes**

The shells are shuffled, **nothing** under any.

And **now** who runs the show
when the show runs them?

    In the long run watch
        the mountebanks' parade.

Then the **stooges** enter unannounced.
No need to hail the defeated.

        And what else is on offer?

Colin Campbell Robinson
13.

Make mountains ring,
make angels cry.

Make angels ring,
make mountains cry.

14.

Footnotes From History

what better place
to hide the prisoner
than in full view
of the authorities

In **dim light** mistakes can be made.

Several pieces play out at once.

He founded a movement
for the purpose of provocation.

He succeeded in blaming those
with perfect alibis.

The flames licked the embassy dry.

And then he disappeared,
because he was never here.

Colin Campbell Robinson

15.

where everyone lies, no one lies; where everything is a lie, nothing is a lie.
– Danilo Kis

How many accidental deaths does it take? How many autopsies?

The knife lies and Doctor Benway signs the certificate. All the experts line up and applaud.

Footnotes From History

The dead are safe at least.
Their bodies carefully prepared for
damnation. They rise as one and sing a
carnival tune as they've been taught to do.

The appropriation: *burning dreams and visions*.

Blown up by bitter methods at speed.
Cold air whisks through an open door.

We could hear the whirring of a singular aim: the
static of disruption from afar.
It was over in moments as *the end* usually comes.

Colin Campbell Robinson

16.

Who conducts the dirty war, **who** conducts the clean?

Where are **the righteous,** in the gutter or the pulpit?

Footnotes From History

When did the **songs of praise** turn into
                                     marching tunes?

Who pays for victors? **Who** accepts defeat?

What year of the Lord is this? Which year of **forgiveness?**

And in the valley, he waits, in a land of storms.

Colin Campbell Robinson
17.

those whose killings are arranged by supposed terrorists are not chosen without reason; but it is generally impossible to be sure of knowing these reasons.
- **Guy Debord**

A theatre, a concert, a sporting event;
these words are written on 9th
November 2015, in a brown notepad miles
away.

Footnotes From History

The meaning's in the moment
but then you're always **there**.

Moving around proves you're living. How long,
there's **nothing** else to do.

Up the M5,
      along the A3,
      around the seventh **roundabout**
and if there's no traffic soon you're **there**
at a destination, then you can enjoy
what's on offer,
         tonight.

Colin Campbell Robinson

**A theatre, a concert, a sporting event
and the special fireworks.**

Moving around and you're dying; who can predict
the next black hole.

We live and die at the confluence of mysteries.

Hidden interests sup **our nous.**
Knowing what we think, **knowing** what we
know, we no longer think.

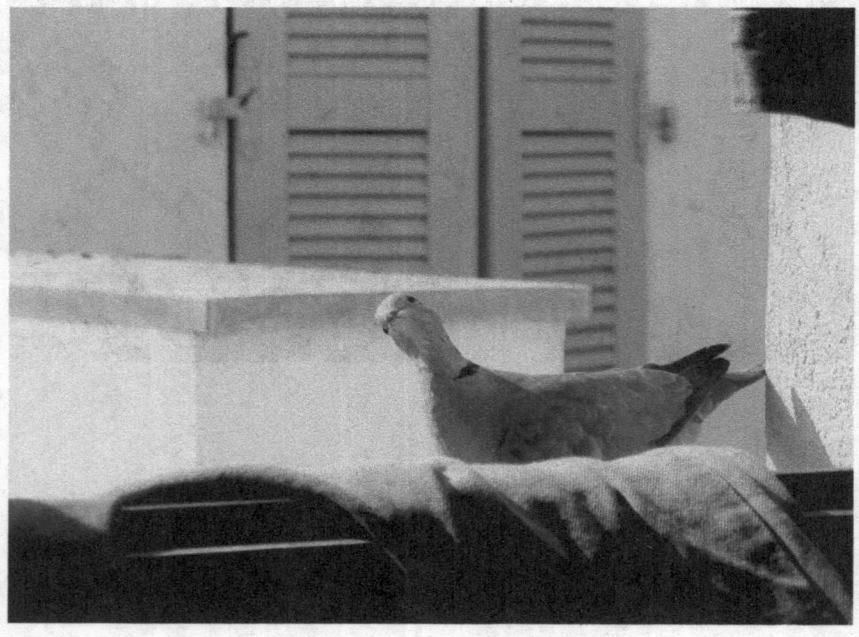

Red poppies in every lapel,
yellow stars on every garment.
Always marked as in or out.

Footnotes From History

The usual suspects fail to make the line up. They're
on other *business,* none of their *business.*

And in other news.

The palace stages its own coup.

The prime minister falls on a sword.

The Bishop of Contraire issues an infallible edict.

The detective inspector inspects the remains.

The innocent confess they were behind the plot.

Nothing is true, everything permissible,
says the Old Man as he despatches his
hashishin, high on dreams of paradise.

Colin Campbell Robinson
REVERB.

under the street
    the beach

(on a wall Paris 68,
grandfather Benjamin
long gone)

viva bohemia
on the shore

there was too much
too be tied   too so little

the petit class
won't set you free

the dealer
and the dealt
can never feel
the felt

do not be thwarted
        he whispered

obstacles scattered
       tripping
       stumbling
         falling

Footnotes From History

conspiring to be part
of the conspiracy
        to undo

he watched and listened
but no one saw
        or heard

the stations of the cross
have been visited
it doesn't take long
        it took so long

yet   the return is sweeter
for all the   bitter days

no more dives (divas)

*

what is seen
    was seen
and it was to be
some/times

when one thing is read
      years ago
and then is performed
        what is this (clairvoyance?)

rambling shamans
in bohemia

Colin Campbell Robinson
NOTES.

[1.] absent self … self absence … self as absence et al can be viewed (heard) in both positive and negative ways (in the electrical sense). to disappear, to not be present; to roll the rock; similarly provocative.

[2.] listening to candyman on the late night tales. might never come back at all, that is total absence of the self having left the self to pacify an-other desire, or then there is leaving (becoming absent) of the irrelevant self i.e. that which does not live in the way or is not in the way.

[3.] Bohemia is where we live wherever that may be (but it must be Bohemia) a place where everything is free and nought constrained; a tolerant space filled with JOY.

[4.] within the words are all the words.

www.ingramcontent.com/pod-product-compliance
Lightning Source LLC
Chambersburg PA
CBHW011803040426
42450CB00018B/3456